M000190303

Ex Libris

Only in the present moment
can we touch life
and be deeply alive.

Each moment is a chance for us

to make peace with the world.

The world needs our happiness.

Only in

the present

moment

can we

touch life

and be

deeply alive.

Our practice is

to live our daily lives

in such a way

that every moment,

every act, becomes

an act of love.

There is no distinction between means and ends.

There is no way to happiness; happiness is the way.

Taking steps

in mindfulness

is an act of liberation.

There is no way to enlightenment;

enlightenment is the way.

Each moment is a chance for us
to make peace with the world.

The world needs our happiness.

Only in

the present

moment

can we

touch life

and be

deeply alive.

The world of peace and joy is at our fingertips.

We only need to touch it.

Learning how
to live deeply
each moment
of our daily life
is our true
practice.

Our practice is

to live our daily lives

in such a way

that every moment,

every act, becomes

an act of love.

There is no distinction between means and ends.

There is no way to happiness; happiness is the way.

Taking steps

in mindfulness

is an act of liberation.

There is no way to enlightenment;

enlightenment is the way.

Each moment is a chance for us

to make peace with the world.

The world needs our happiness.

Only in

the present

moment

can we

touch life

and be

deeply alive.

The world of peace and joy is at our fingertips.

We only need to touch it.

Learning how

to live deeply

each moment

of our daily life

is our true

practice.

Our practice is

to live our daily lives

in such a way

that every moment,

every act, becomes

an act of love.

There is no distinction between means and ends.

There is no way to happiness; happiness is the way.

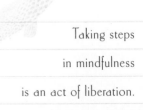

Taking steps

in mindfulness

is an act of liberation.

There is no way to enlightenment;

enlightenment is the way.

Each moment is a chance for us
to make peace with the world.

The world needs our happiness.

Only in

the present

moment

can we

touch life

and be

deeply alive.

The world of peace and joy is at our fingertips.

We only need to touch it.

Learning how

to live deeply

each moment

of our daily life

is our true

practice.

Our practice is

to live our daily lives

in such a way

that every moment,

every act, becomes

an act of love.

There is no distinction between means and ends.

There is no way to happiness; happiness is the way.

Taking steps

in mindfulness

is an act of liberation.

There is no way to enlightenment;

enlightenment is the way.

Each moment is a chance for us
to make peace with the world.

The world needs our happiness.

Only in

the present

moment

can we

touch life

and be

deeply alive.

The world of peace and joy is at our fingertips.

We only need to touch it.

Learning how

to live deeply

each moment

of our daily life

is our true

practice.

Our practice is

to live our daily lives

in such a way

that every moment,

every act, becomes

an act of love.

There is no distinction between means and ends.

There is no way to happiness; happiness is the way.

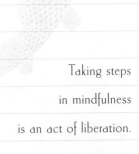

Taking steps

in mindfulness

is an act of liberation.

There is no way to enlightenment;

enlightenment is the way.

Each moment is a chance for us

to make peace with the world.

The world needs our happiness.

Only in

the present

moment

can we

touch life

and be

deeply alive.

The world of peace and joy is at our fingertips.

We only need to touch it.

Learning how

to live deeply

each moment

of our daily life

is our true

practice.

Our practice is

to live our daily lives

in such a way

that every moment,

every act, becomes

an act of love.

There is no distinction between means and ends.

There is no way to happiness; happiness is the way.

Taking steps

in mindfulness

is an act of liberation.

There is no way to enlightenment;

enlightenment is the way.

Each moment is a chance for us

to make peace with the world.

The world needs our happiness.

Only in

the present

moment

can we

touch life

and be

deeply alive.

The world of peace and joy is at our fingertips.

We only need to touch it.

Learning how

to live deeply

each moment

of our daily life

is our true

practice.

Our practice is

to live our daily lives

in such a way

that every moment,

every act, becomes

an act of love.

There is no distinction between means and ends.

There is no way to happiness; happiness is the way.

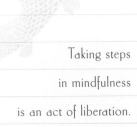

Taking steps

in mindfulness

is an act of liberation.

There is no way to enlightenment;

enlightenment is the way.

Each moment is a chance for us
to make peace with the world.

The world needs our happiness.

Only in

the present

moment

can we

touch life

and be

deeply alive.

The world of peace and joy is at our fingertips.

We only need to touch it.

Learning how

to live deeply

each moment

of our daily life

is our true

practice.

Our practice is

to live our daily lives

in such a way

that every moment,

every act, becomes

an act of love.

There is no distinction between means and ends.

There is no way to happiness; happiness is the way.

Taking steps

in mindfulness

is an act of liberation.

There is no way to enlightenment;

enlightenment is the way.

Each moment is a chance for us
to make peace with the world.

The world needs our happiness.

Only in

the present

moment

can we

touch life

and be

deeply alive.

The world of peace and joy is at our fingertips.

We only need to touch it.

Learning how

to live deeply

each moment

of our daily life

is our true

practice.

Our practice is

to live our daily lives

in such a way

that every moment,

every act, becomes

an act of love.

There is no distinction between means and ends.

There is no way to happiness; happiness is the way.

Taking steps

in mindfulness

is an act of liberation.

There is no way to enlightenment;

enlightenment is the way.

Each moment is a chance for us
to make peace with the world.

The world needs our happiness.

Only in

the present

moment

can we

touch life

and be

deeply alive.

The world of peace and joy is at our fingertips.

We only need to touch it.

Learning how

to live deeply

each moment

of our daily life

is our true

practice.

Our practice is

to live our daily lives

in such a way

that every moment,

every act, becomes

an act of love.

There is no distinction between means and ends.

There is no way to happiness; happiness is the way.

Taking steps

in mindfulness

is an act of liberation.

There is no way to enlightenment;

enlightenment is the way.

Each moment is a chance for us
to make peace with the world.

The world needs our happiness.

Only in

the present

moment

can we

touch life

and be

deeply alive.

The world of peace and joy is at our fingertips.

We only need to touch it.

Learning how

to live deeply

each moment

of our daily life

is our true

practice.

Our practice is

to live our daily lives

in such a way

that every moment,

every act, becomes

an act of love.

There is no distinction between means and ends.

There is no way to happiness; happiness is the way.

Taking steps

in mindfulness

is an act of liberation.

There is no way to enlightenment;

enlightenment is the way.

Each moment is a chance for us
to make peace with the world.

The world needs our happiness.

Only in

the present

moment

can we

touch life

and be

deeply alive.

The world of peace and joy is at our fingertips.

We only need to touch it.

Learning how

to live deeply

each moment

of our daily life

is our true

practice.

Our practice is

to live our daily lives

in such a way

that every moment,

every act, becomes

an act of love.

There is no distinction between means and ends.

There is no way to happiness; happiness is the way.

Taking steps

in mindfulness

is an act of liberation.

There is no way to enlightenment;

enlightenment is the way.

Each moment is a chance for us
to make peace with the world.

The world needs our happiness.

Only in

the present

moment

can we

touch life

and be

deeply alive.

The world of peace and joy is at our fingertips.

We only need to touch it.

Learning how

to live deeply

each moment

of our daily life

is our true

practice.

Our practice is

to live our daily lives

in such a way

that every moment,

every act, becomes

an act of love.

There is no distinction between means and ends.

There is no way to happiness; happiness is the way.

Taking steps

in mindfulness

is an act of liberation.

There is no way to enlightenment;

enlightenment is the way.

Each moment is a chance for us
to make peace with the world.

The world needs our happiness.

Only in

the present

moment

can we

touch life

and be

deeply alive.

Learning how

to live deeply

each moment

of our daily life

is our true

practice.

Our practice is

to live our daily lives

in such a way

that every moment,

every act, becomes

an act of love.

There is no distinction between means and ends.

There is no way to happiness; happiness is the way.

Taking steps

in mindfulness

is an act of liberation.

There is no way to enlightenment;

enlightenment is the way.